# AN ALPHABET OF STORMS
## Henry Normal

Flapjack Press

flapjackpress.co.uk

Exploring the synergy between performance and the page

Published in 2025 by Flapjack Press
Salford, Gtr Manchester
⊕ flapjackpress.co.uk · ▶ flapjackpress2520
f flapjackpress · 𝕏 flapjackpress

ISBN 978-1-0686052-6-0

Cover art by Johnny Carroll-Pell
f Art By Johnny · ⊙ johnnycarrollpell

Author photo by Richard Davis
f Richard Davis Photography · 𝕏 WiredDavis
⊙ richarddavismcrphotography

Printed by Imprint Digital
Exeter, Devon
⊕ digital.imprint.co.uk

FSC

MANCHESTER
A UNESCO City
of Literature

northern
fiction
alliance

*Dedicated to Richard Davis,*
*a great friend, an inspiration,*
*and a brilliant photographer.*

*With thanks to Linda Hallam, Paul Neads,*
*Richard Davis, Angela Pell, and Johnny Carroll-Pell.*

# Contents

An Alphabet of Storms

## Empire of Rain

Rain by its very nature
is temporary
and generally commonplace

Only too much
or too little
draws particular attention

We name storms
but raindrops are too many
to personalise

One spot on its own
might not be considered
rain at all

At first we say not that
it is raining
but that it is trying to rain

Only when the individual
is joined by others
has it succeeded

If poets should strike –
a world without similes
what would it be like?

Imagine a world
without verse. I can't think of
a thing not as good

Imagine a world
without images. I can't
think of anything

## The Secret Diary of Henry Normal, Aged 68½

*(where I put my secret innermost thoughts, display my sensitivity, and expose the tenderness behind the enigmatic smile)*


Dear Diary
Arrived at the gig
What a shithole

The audience look like the walking dead
I've seen yogurt with more life

I'll not sell a single book tonight to these tight bastards
(Am I oversharing?)

Don't know if I can bear trudging through another show
parroting these tired old poems
plastering a fake smile on my face
disguising weak old jokes as art

The night lies before me like the seventh circle of Hell

(Sorry, that was yesterday's entry
at Peterborough

It all makes sense now

Here's today's entry)

Dear Diary
What a great place. Lovely audience
Very astute
Probably get a standing ovation tonight
Sell a load of books
Just need to start well

## A Non-Contentious Letter

Dear Sir / Madam / non-binary / trans / other

I hope you / they / he / she / them are well / managing / coping

There has been an error / mistake / confusion

So I'm returning the thesaurus / book of synonyms and antonyms / lists of similar words

## A Scientist Speaks to His Wife

What existed before the Big Bang? Nothing?
Or everything that now exists just waiting to begin
all crammed in to the head of a pin?
If so, what was this pin floating in?

And if the universe is expanding
as scientists say is true
what
is it expanding into?

Scientists and philosophers believe
there is no such thing as nothing
That is to say 'non-being'
the opposite of something
the antithesis of everything

They say there is no such thing as an empty room
no such thing as a true vacuum

Even a vacuum has virtual particles
and will carry light and gravity
quarks, neutrinos and even string
if you believe in String Theory

By its very definition nothing doesn't exist
It's a state that has never been
So when you say 'Our love was nothing'
what exactly do you mean?

I remember how carefully
you caressed at first

You adorned me in wallpaper
to protect me

Your first words were so
delicate and perfect

You would share your thoughts with me
before anyone else

Then you noticed
no matter how gently you pressed

indentations could be seen
on the reverse of the page

You preferred the virgin
side of me

Your words became
looser and more casual

Lines were abandoned
edges became frayed

At the heart of me
pages were torn out

Corners turned down
my spine bent and broken

Sentences became scribbles
drawings just doodles

and when I was all used up
you disposed of me

without a thought

Got yourself a new jotter
Started the process again

## John the Baptist of Housework

Get up early
Plenty to do
No time to rest
The cleaner is due

Hang up the coats
Stow each shoe
Clothes off the floor
The cleaner is due

Fold the towels
Double-flush the loo
Straighten the duvet
The cleaner is due

Load washing machine
The dishwasher too
Tidy the table
The cleaner is due

Now act calm
with a casual air
and say 'excuse the mess'
when the cleaner appears

## Redistribution

I've stray hairs in my ears
grey hairs on my legs
I've hair there and everywhere
except the top of my head

I'm hirsute in my hooter
my nostrils are like forests
If nose hairs were azaleas
I could open up a florist's

And when I visit the barber
I'm left with no pretensions
He takes the strands from my tabs
and uses them for extensions

Whenever I need my back washed
my wife tells me the truth
She says I look a lot like Sasquatch
but with a new sun roof

Each fold is full of follicles
Each crevice has curls to be cut
I'm running out of Vosene
every time I wash my butt

I've got plaits under my arms
I've got bangs between each toe
And even though it's un-PC
my pubes are now an Afro

She looked for love
but in the wrong place

Under the oceans
and out into space

Down a microscope
in life's smallest trace

In misshapen vegetables
with a funny face

But only met men
She wanted to mace

## Even Poets Find It Hard to Say I Love You

Another day without kisses
or the touch of your warm skin

I am marooned
in routine

The getting on with it
and the getting through

Every night I light a bonfire
and pray to the moon

to feel your eyes
meet mine

to share a heartbeat
across the room

or to spoon as lovers do
and breathe you in once more

I've fallen for my Doctor
Her bedside manner's inviting
She wrote me a love letter
but I couldn't read the writing

I confessed my heart burned for her
I professed the pain was real
She told me to take Gaviscon
after every meal

'No' I said 'I've fallen for you'
She didn't flinch at all
She looked at my age and said
'You mean you've had a fall?'

She refused to treat me differently
I should have seen that as a warning
She would only accept my phone calls
at 8.30 in the morning

I complained I'd die without her
To see her this minute was a must
She arranged a consultation
for the back end of August

I got an emergency appointment
to convince her love could bloom
She said she was seeing someone
and would I sit in the waiting room

I declared only she could cure me
Having seen her I could never go
She prescribed me Syrup of Figs
for a couple of days or so

'If you think we're well suited
you must be mad' she said
I demanded a second opinion
She said 'You're off your bleeding head'

I'd become terminally love sick
A delusion I need to resist
But luckily it's true love this time
now I'm seeing a specialist

## The Young Crony

I kept my head down
I did what I was told
I avoided crime
I bided my time
I used to be so old

I never questioned my betters
I wouldn't be so bold
I watched the clock
I tugged my forelock
I used to be so old

Nose to the grindstone
I longed for life to unfold
I believed all was fine
I towed the party line
I used to be so old

I steered clear of trouble
I was easily controlled
A blink of the eye
and life's gone by
I used to be so old

## Charmageddon

I've overdosed
on being the host

I do like a guest
but I like a rest
the best

It's lovely
to have people stay
but lovelier
when they go away

I don't give a fig for a big shindig
I don't give a fanny for a hootenanny
a mass clambake can be a mistake
a vast hoedown can fast go down
a fulsome bacchanalia can end in failure
a jumbo jamboree is not for me

Remember it's well dumb
to outstay your welcome

You know you should retire
when I warm my pyjamas by the fire

# I Said to Ange ...

'I hope I die first
That would be the biz
cos I don't really know
where anything is

Making funeral arrangements
is not really me
I'm much better
at the RIP

I hope I'm first to pop
I'm just not good at ends
And I wouldn't be much cop
at talking to your friends

No, all said and done' I said
'I should be first to go'
And Ange said to me
'Oh, I do hope so'

## The Lighting of a Candle

I know there is no magic
in the lighting of a candle
for the departed

Or if there is
it is within
the person who makes the gesture

Still I'm drawn to this symbolism
though the life of a single candle
is short

Perhaps because the life
of a single candle is short
and the nature of the flame
so vulnerable

The lighting of a candle
is a prayer
a celebration
a declaration

Fleeting as it is
the moment is a defiance
to all that is dark

## I'm Fairly Sure I've Spent ...

more time correcting
the autocorrect than it's
ever saved me

## The Threads of My Life Are ...

starting to unravel
a bald patch on my gravel
impedes my travel

## To Anyone Who's Ever Made a Mistake

Some falter and fall
Some make a wrong call
Some hope to avoid all the damage
Some neglect or forget
Some dodge unpaid debt
Some carry regret as baggage

Some mistakes are unfair
Some lose faith in prayer
Some curse their disadvantage
Some collapse or collide
Some slither and slide
Some wither inside of a marriage

Some strike out in pain
Some insult their own brain
Some cannot restrain the savage
Some attempt to stay true
Some still go askew
Some somehow get through and manage

## Ignorance

A fly has entered my room
by a side window

It keeps bashing itself against
the main pane to escape

It must be aware of the open window
it came in through

I can see it
and I've only got two eyes

It's obviously struggling
with the concept of glass

You would think the movement of air
would draw its attention

but no
it bangs into the glass again and again

I try to shoo it towards freedom
with a book

It's having none of it
and simply flies higher

I'm not as fast as a fly
even with two books

although the constant impacts
of brain on glass

will soon slow it down
and I can then lift it

from the window ledge
with a single sheet of paper

I've no wish to see it
come to harm

I open more windows
to increase its chances

whilst risking
further insects entering

I close the curtains
to restrict its options and wait

The fabric breathes in and out
with the breeze

## Seniors' Special

'What are WE having for breakfast?'
the young waiter loudly snorts
I said 'I don't know about you
but I'm having homicidal thoughts

I think I'll pass on being patronised
the pity and disdain
Ageism is no way to start the day
so shall WE begin again?

I'll offer YOU a choice of breakfast
I'll raise MY voice to ensure you're hearing it
Serve breakfast without being condescending
or you may just end up wearing it'

## The Party Line

Let's throw a party called life
invite the world and his wife
like a Hollywood premiere screening
It'll all be fine
I'll bring the wine
and you bring the meaning

Let's invite the folks next door
outlaw all war
they'll thank us for intervening
Ignore the reaction
I'll bring distraction
and you bring the meaning

Let's embrace all humanity
put an end to insanity
all the world convening
everything worked out
I'll bring my doubt
and you bring the meaning

Let's open our tired eyes
expose a trillion lies
the insults so demeaning
I pray we can cope
I'll bring the hope
and you bring the meaning

## Existential Dreadline

*(or 'The End is Half-Past Nigh')*

The end of the world is annoying
Why doesn't everyone shout it?
Everything is going wrong
and it's taking its time about it

## The Tortured Poets Department Replies

As attention doth drift
the gift of Swift
I fear doth fail her
I remain a fan of Jonathan
more than Taylor

## Poem to Help You Avoid Procrastination

I'll do that one later

## Cohabiting with Jack Frost
*(or 'The Artic Home Keys')*

According to my windows
there's proof without a doubt
Condensation outside shows
it's colder in that out

I've snowdrifts up my stairs
I should swiftly plough a path
I've chilblains on my armchairs
a polar bear in my bath

I've defrosted the kitchen floor
covered the carpets with grit
stuck a sign by the front door
'Wipe boots before you exit'

The snowman on the sofa said
'Now's not the time to panic'
but there's an iceberg in my bed
could scupper the Titanic

I've secured a small loan
to switch on the gas a smidge
although when inside alone
I warm myself by the fridge

I've huskies in my hallway
icicles by the recycling bin
Time to de-ice my duvet
my home's warmer out than in

## Monday

The weekend is done day
Put away the fun day
Working week begun day
Fire the starting gun day

## Tuesday

Not a day I'd choose day
Nothing to enthuse day
Look down at my shoes day
Avoid getting a bruise day

## Wednesday

It sort of depends day
Let's see what fate sends day
Go slow on the bends day
Let's see how it ends day

## Thursday

Not the worst day
Not an averse day
At the mercy of the universe day
Maybe tighten your purse day

## Friday

Don't expect a reply day
Didn't the week fly by day
Afternoon like a sigh day
An early goodbye day

**Saturday**

Plenty of chatter day
Mad as a hatter day
Restraint doesn't matter day
Anything else is a flatter day

**Sunday**

A walk don't run day
Set the phasers to stun day
Nothing needs to be done day
I'll come to terms with it one day

## I Don't Think I've Got Another Password in Me

You won't accept my password
You say it needs to be better
I need a symbol and a number
and at least one capital letter

You *still* won't accept my password
It's less than 20 digits long
So I've decided to change it to
Stickitupyour*rsehole1

So
I tap it in and up you chime
You say
I had that one last time

The engine can't quite make the slope
There's steeper climbs and little hope
The driver's state is not ideal
Asleep at the wheel

The train may never reach the top
The gears grind, the pistons stop
The driver's loss hard to conceal
Asleep at the wheel

The brakes won't hold out for long
This deadweight is far too strong
The pull of solid steel
Asleep at the wheel

The stars shine down indifferent
The driver in his firmament
ignores our sad appeal
Asleep at the wheel

## Orange – Almost My Favourite Colour

The colour of sunshine
Yam and cantaloupe
An apricot or mango
Butternut squash soup

A Monarch butterfly
Kumquat and peach
Tangerines or clementines
Basketball for the beach

Stripes on a clown fish
Stripes on a tiger
Marigolds, pumpkins
The flames of a fire

An airplane's black box
making it easy to trace
Donald Trump's
big stupid face

Some of us were born in winter
and in winter we will die
We live our lives outside your door
far from your warm fireside

Some of us were born in war
and in war we will die
We bury our dreams somewhere safe
beneath the fear we hide

Some of us were born unwashed
and unwashed we will die
We clean our kids as best we can
with the tears our parents cried

Some of us were born unwanted
and unwanted we will die
We live our lives outside your door
and are seldom let inside

## Poetry is a Breeze

*(aka 'Gusty Springfield')*

I wanted to write up a storm
a cyclone worthy of my craft
a tornado, a blizzard, a hurricane
so here's a first draught

## Anticipating

*(a rhyme-ku)*

I find the great thing
about anticipating
is in the                                    waiting

## Steamed Granules of Rolled Semolina

As enticing as rice
at quite a nice price
couscous –
so good they named it twice

## Optimism and the Second Law of Thermodynamics

Objects appear to spin secure in space
as energy and mass compete
but with time all worlds will turn to waste
empires crumbling beneath our feet

The universe tends towards disorder
all change more trick than treat
chaos lies around the corner
undeterred by self-deceit

You know no dollar will deny death
fame and power are a fickle conceit
so you pray with every given breath
that the truth is incomplete

No-one can paint out tomorrow
nor create Heaven as concrete
yet still you refuse to reside in sorrow
and choose hope with each heartbeat

Driving from Hastings
to Angela's mum's in Seaford
the devastation
from over 70,000 tons of bombs
lies all around us

By the time we reach Bexhill
we have seen nearly 15,000 dead children

Driving past Eastbourne
9,500 dead women stare
back at us

Coming through Alfriston
over 157,000 buildings
lie destroyed

Hastings to Seaford
is about the same distance
as the length of the Gaza Strip

The journey takes us an hour
in my car
On a stretch of motorway
it would take less than 25 minutes

There's more people in Gaza
than in East Sussex
but in an area
5 times smaller
(not as long and not as wide)

The density of population in Gaza
before the conflict
was akin to that of London

but most have now been squeezed
into an area even smaller
and squeezed again
into an area even smaller
than that

Arriving at Seaford
over 1.9 million
displaced people greet us
whilst the half a million
with no homes to return to
carry what they can

Angela's mum makes us lunch
as hundreds of thousands
starve through no fault of their own

This afternoon I will drive back
the 25 miles

past all the faces once again

## Worry

Some worries sit at the back of your mind
like a half-eaten meal in the fridge

Some worries come and go like a spot on your chin
They fade and disappear often even from memory

Other worries breeze in and out like the weather
They may return with the change of seasons

Some live with you like lodgers
that you know are up to no good

Some you carry in you like an unborn twin

## Biopic for a Myopic

I fell for a girl in glasses
but my love was unrequited
She couldn't see
a life with me
she was obviously shortsighted

To her I was a blur
that was her description
She said I looked strange
things needed to change
then arranged a new prescription

She married her optician
She was nothing if not thrifty
An easy decision
she saw with precision
now her vision was fifty-fifty

But he pulled the wool over her eyes
he never loved her at all
What with the fighting
and the blindsiding
she couldn't see the writing on the wall

When I think of her cruel words
I still bear the scars
Though it cuts to the quick
I'm still lovesick
for the girl with the thick jam jars

I bumped into her last week
it seems she still lives 'local'
To my surprise
she's seeing guys
but identifies as bi-focal

## Lime-ku

'The wall needs pointing'
I say, pointing at the wall
where it needs pointing


## Bird Hide-ku

Nature spied outside
Folk inside un-spied / otherwise
it is not a hide


## Automatic Tanka

Automatic cars
like automatic writing
are fine, but you still

have to be there to make the
whole automatic thing work

## The Portal

Once inside the library doors
I escaped and changed
and travelled through time and space
all at the turn of a page

Met kings and prisoners
heroes and villains
wise men and fools
giants and those forgotten

I explored the remotest peaks
discovered hidden deserts
the bottom of the deepest sea
and the moons of imagined planets

I became an animal, an insect
a bird, a spirit, an alien
a creature long dead
and a creature yet to be born

I flew and leapt
and dived and swam
and cried and laughed
and loved and felt love in return

I learnt from a million minds
the lessons of a million lives
and of those who
died a million times
to save these worlds for you

## Library Tickets

The very first official papers
I remember owning
with my name on it
were my library tickets

I was five and they were pink
and more than anything
each ticket was a certificate for
self-determination

I could choose
  Where I wanted my imagination to go
  Who I wanted to journey with
  How fast I wanted to travel
  What I wanted to learn and
  When I wanted change direction

I could choose
  Not my teachers
  Not my parents
  Not a politician
  The five-year-old me

As I grew older
I graduated to green tickets –
like Certificates of Adulthood
Each ticket a licence to explore
and I could now read any book in the library
any book I wanted to read

Later, of course, I found
I had other official paperwork

I had a birth certificate
that confirmed who I was

I obtained a driving licence
that confirmed who I was

And I obtained a passport
that confirmed who I was

But the library tickets were
special

They were a passport
to who I could be

## Making Pot Holes into Poet Holes?

Will councils compound Pound to save pounds?
Slash cash with Ogden Nash?
Level Larkin for level parkin'?
Landfill Lord Tennyson like trash?

Will they fill the floor with Evelyn Waugh?
Eliot and Auden and many more?
Combine Rupi Kaur with Hardy
to invent Rupi Hardcore?

On motorways Wordsworth's literary wealth
will they lay, with poets even older?
And to the side Shakespeare himself
on what they may call the 'Bard Shoulder'?

Are wheels in motion for wheels over Andrew Motion?
Will they bury Berryman before their Donne?
Will we see more ridges over Robert Seymour Bridges?
Your tyre on Lord Byron for fun?

Will Concrete Poetry in craters creep?
John 'Bitumen' everywhere you see?
With my books in a dip particularly deep
to reflect my poetry?

## Carlton Rd Library in the 1960s

It was just round the corner
from our house
but a million miles away

The first time I went in
my legs weren't that much
longer than my short trousers

It was like a church
quiet and atmospheric
or a bank
respectful and businesslike
or a school
formal but friendly

It was huge
and clean
and ordered
and it smelt
of books
and polish

And I felt I needed to be
on my best behaviour
with clean hands
and shirt tucked in

I needed to live up
to this building

And each time I went in
I grew taller
and taller
and taller

## Going Out

Ange always wants me to take her out

but I'm happy where I am

I said 'You went out on Monday'

She said 'That was a mammogram'


## Plants Love Music

To help it grow
I played my plant Coldplay
It quickly grew two legs
and moved two doors away


## The Four Seasons
*(reinterpreted)*

To really capture the four seasons
Vivaldi ought
to make winter very long
and summer far too short

## A Proper Job

I can't relax
with workmen at my house

I feel I should be engaged in something
more substantial

as if I'd be doing
the job they're doing

If only I hadn't this other
more important task to complete

not just scribbling nonsense
or looking for a rhyme for discombobulated

My eyelids would prefer sleep
but I need to keep a vigil

for teas and coffees
and other essential amenities

I've moved rooms to hide
I tell myself I need quiet to create

then look down at the page
at the true benefit of this solitude

I'm failing to compete
with a valid version of myself

as a writer of worth
Discombobulated

with chance of rhyming
risk unmodulated

## The Baker's Lament

She was the best thing since sliced bread
the baker said

She took the trophy
on matters loafy

She was more fun than a buttered bun
more posh than fresh brioche
better yet than a baked baguette
She was just the job like a crusty cob

She had more charm than a barm
more glow than sourdough
more soul than a wholewheat roll

She was everything I'd ever want
So much more than a warm croissant

or for that matter
a hot ciabatta

And was not as fickle as a pumpernickel
less plain than a multigrain
less bitter than a pitta
not as thick as a French stick

She was in my every plan which
involved a sandwich

Though naïve in love
I gave her my upmost
I stood too close to her flame
and ended up toast

But then – Heaven
She had eleven
sisters and a cousin
making in all a baker's dozen

## Tanglewood

When sycamores mesh
vertical is just one growth
option it appears

Messing the hedgerows
wildflowers eke out sunlight
rhododendrons choke

Hacking through thistles
or nettles in tiny shorts
not recommended

## Burning Old Newspapers

Facts and theories
given their final twist as
fears fly off in flames

E x a g g e r a t i o n s
Scares and scandals scorch and curl
Boasts blacken and shrink

Self-importance and
self-indulgence crumble and
turn back into smoke

## I Can Hear the Dishwasher Whispering

Sun spotlights the floor
through the kitchen roof window
throwing angled shapes

It is not that I
am afraid things will go wrong
I know that they will

It's I'm afraid of
my inability to
put them right again

and the thought they will
always be diminished
due mainly to me

My anxiety
hides smartly under my hair
and beneath my clothes

It knows if it was
in the open I'd do more
to get rid of it

There are rooms in my
house where my feet never tread
Some views left unseen

## If Only I Had an Official Self-Diagnosis

I wouldn't have to feel so bad
about my lack of interest in others
or remember the names of people's kids
or their kids' fathers and mothers

## Deconstruction Haiku

Five syllables then
add seven more syllables
then five syllables

## Interior Design

Fashions repeat
So I've found
swivel chairs
will come back round

## Scary Thoughts

What you are wearing when you die
is how you will appear as a ghost
So try not to exit on the toilet
with your trousers round your toes

And men – in case you croak in bed
make sure you've not forgotten
no matter how hot it is
to put on your pyjama bottoms

Try not to die in a sleep mask
Try not to die in the bath
Try not to die wearing a face pack
or your partner's pants for a laugh

Running a marathon may be risky
dressed as a pantomime horse
and the last thing we want for Christmas
is an exorcism on Santa Claus

A phantom face-painted with a flag
you may prefer to give a miss
And no-one should spend the afterlife
as part of a tribute band to Kiss

Don't die wearing fancy dress
be careful the costume you've chosen
No-one needs to be haunted
by a bloke dressed as Elsa from *Frozen*

## Family Photo

We have very few photos of us altogether
Usually one of us is taking the picture
Thank goodness for selfies

We have very few photos of us
all looking at camera
and smiling

We have very few photos
where we all look reasonable
where lighting has been kind

The rarity adds more value
if you can add value
to priceless

## French Kissing a Dentist

I fell in love with a dentist
It didn't last that long
Whenever we French kissed
she'd check for cavities with her tongue

I fell in love with a dentist
She was such a tease
Whilst we French kissed
she'd check for gum disease

I fell in love with a dentist
Her sense of humour was droll
After we French kissed
she'd say 'Now spit in the bowl'

I fell in love with a dentist
Always working – whatever she did
Every time we French kissed
she'd charge me sixty quid

### a. Country Vet

I fell in love with a country vet
but her touch just sent me numb
As the image I could never forget
was her arm up a cow's bum

### b. Fishmonger

I fell in love with a fishmonger
knowing one wrong word could kill it
I said 'I have a fish-shaped hole in my life
and I want you to fillet'

### c. Clairvoyant

I fell in love with a clairvoyant
who lived beneath a steeple
But whenever we were alone
she was seeing other people

### d. Tattooist

I fell in love with a tattooist
who slept holding a pin
In the morning I realised
she had designs on my skin

### e. Juggler

I fell in love with a juggler
I didn't need pressure like that
She said she would leave me
at the drop of a hat

## Weeding Rhymes with Bleeding

I'm in a bind with bindweed
Creeping Charlie drives me crazy
crabgrass makes me crabby
don't dare mention the daisy

A thistle makes me bristle
ragwort I find trying
There's nothing dandy
about the dandelion

I've got clover all over
nettles that sting
dock leaves and buttercups
happily doing their thing

I've been weeks on my knees
I could have weeded longer
No matter how many hours spent
the buggers come back stronger

A weed is just a flower
in the wrong place it's said
Maybe it's me that's
in the wrong place instead

## A Small Cross in the Wild Grass

Dark blue moves slowly and surely
from sea to ocean

as tankers and container ships
scab the horizon

Sunshine visits the coast
like an old friend
who can't stop long

In the distance
dogs exercise their owners

There's a different flag
on the crumbling church

Closer to
I can hear birds improvising
in the hawthorn bushes

I've spent my whole life
visiting nature
as though other

Now the pulse behind my eyes
mocks a countdown

I'm relearning to walk uphill

Someone has gone to
some trouble to mark
their father
with a small cross
in the wild grass

All the words
on all the benches
can't contain the grief

A cold northerly bites
the back of my hands

I look down
and a little creature lands
on my phone whilst I type

I blow it gently
Let no one die today

## A Teacher's Warning

With maths homework
nothing is too complex f'
a crafty kid in a room
alone with an Alexa

## Rhyl

Rain on a caravan roof
There's no sound like it
Nature in all its glory
washing off seagull shit

## Poem Listing the Complete Benefits of Brexit

## Serious Poetry Society Manifesto

Shun fun
before it's begun

Never experiment
with merriment

Frivolity
is not our policy

Jolly
is folly

Mirth
keep a wide berth

If you're looking for a laugh
you've made a gaff

If you seek to be amused
you're excused

Looking for the craic
don't come back

There's a reason why 'enjoying'
rhymes with 'annoying'

If you need entertaining
I'm done explaining

## Prime Ordeal

I've booked an Amazon funeral
so the hole they need to dig
will have to be much larger
as the box is far too big

I'm opting for an open coffin
so you can see my face
and to ensure Amazon haven't
sent me to the wrong place

Don't worry about the transit
I shall be having a lovely nap
on my way to Heaven
surrounded by bubble wrap

## Alchemy

Dusk in mid-December
and the trees have turned to rust
Smoke from my boiler
merges with the mist

We're winter-warming the globe
breathing out greenhouse gasses
turning over diesel
toasting from plastic glasses

We're churning worry to cancer
doomscrolling instant news
recycling recycled waste
autocorrecting our views

Some rotate in unseen graves
in curves some crash and burn
In this modern half-life
no-one knows where to turn

Revolutions roll and twist
and muscles turn to mush
This ever-increasing spiral
may well see the end of us

But though tired faces turn off
and the young in turn turn old
Earth still spins upon her axis
as the sunset turns to gold

## Morning Dew on Cobwebs in the Hedge

Plant life and creatures
conspire with time and weather
to create beauty

## The Algal Bloom

Want to swim in the May Rot?
You may not
Smells like veg gone bad
feels a tad like snot

## Tanka-ing Down

Outside my window
raindrops on the scaffolding
wake me from dreamland

Am I being burgled by
a marching timpani band?

## In Love with Night

Shakespeare's moon
is your moon

It's the same moon that shone
on the initial spark of life

The same moon seen
by the first primate to stand tall

The moon that shone down
on Socrates and Sappho

On Moses, Jesus
Mohammed and Buddha

The moon Darwin and Hawkins saw
Turing's and Einstein's moon

Ghandi's and Mandela's moon
Martin Luther King's moon

Tonight
it is our moon

## Questions

Is retirement hard work?
The hours look awfully long
and you're the only boss to blame
when things go terribly wrong

Is getting up tiring?
Then the day all downhill?
Is there enough fun stuff
for afternoons still to fill?

Do you think back fondly
to when time was fleeting
now alone, complaining to yourself
at your annual general meeting?

Do holidays not seem so vital?
Do weekends start to blur?
Does one day look much like the next?
Each year appear to recur?

Do you throw yourself into a hobby
improve your health, DIY your nest?
Then crave an active career
so you can have a rest?

Are you busy waiting for death?
Does life seem sad looking back?
Is retirement your bag?
Or might you give yourself the sack?

## *Answer*

Retired, you find it's hard to believe
anyone ever has time for a job
and there's never enough hours
to answer questions from a nob

## On Reflection

I need to get a new mirror
mine's broken – I should bin it
A miserable old bastard
seems to be living in it

My friend Brian says the bloke
has quite a handsome brow
My wife tells me it's all okay
a patient woman lives there now

I've bought so many mirrors
it can be hard keeping track
and every time I look in one
the miserable bastard's back

Embrace your shadows
Let in all your ghosts
Light the dark corners
that you fear the most

Demons or angels
haunted by regret
The faces of failure
you choose to forget

In midnight's mirror
reflect upon the truth
You bear the soul of
your imperfect youth

Unchain memory
All spirits be seen
You are and will be
more than you have been

## The Serpent's Side of the Story

It'ssss a sssstitch up
I'm innocccccent

Sssso there I am
in the garden of Eden

Ssssoaking up the ssssunshine
ssssome woman ssssidles up to me

Jusssst being neighbourly
I ssssays 'How you doing?'

Sssshe's sssssurprised I can sssspeak

Sssshe's sssssays 'Hey sssserpent
How come you can sssspeak
when none of the other creaturessss can sssspeak?'
(I can't do her voicccce)

Sssso I ssssays 'I ssssucked on that ssssucculent fruit
from the tree of knowledge'

Next thing I know sssshe's having her asssssss
kicked out of Paradisssse

The boyfriend – sssssame ssssituation
I never even ssssspoke to him

I mean God never ssssaid to me
Don't sssssuck on that ssssucculent fruit
He never ssssaid sssshit to me

And he never ssssaid don't ssssay sssshit
about ssssucking on that
sssssucculent fruit sssshit either

And he's omnipressssssent sssso
he sssssaw what was happening

Now God'sssss mad at me, punisssshing me
like he was never there
like he couldn't have ssssstopped it
if he wanted

Sssso now I've got to crawl on my belly
and eat dusssst the ressssst of my dayssss

Sssshit makes no ssssensssse

## Noah's Ark – The True Story

The animals went in two by two
but because of their sexual habits
after 150 days and nights
the Ark was overrun by rabbits


## Methuselah

After 969 years
Methuselah was dead
Despite his longevity
there's nothing more to be said


## Daniel in the Lion's Den – The Lion's Story in Haiku Form

You are what you eat
I'm not eating him / clearly
he's an idiot

## Jonah – The Whale's Version

You'll never guess who I had
in my stomachs the other week
Only this bloke called Jonah
3 days and 3 nights
like a bleedin' Airbnb

I said 'You don't want
to be staying in there too long
There's no air in my stomachs
only gastric juices
that will eat you alive'

He said he was running away from God
I said 'Good luck with that mate
God is omnipresent
He's probably in my stomachs with you'

He said 'How come he don't get eaten
alive with the gastric juices?'
I said 'I don't know mate
He moves in mysterious ways'

Anyway
this Jonah bloke disagreed with me
so I coughed him up on the beach
Turns out they've written a book about him
I get no royalties
Nothing
Unbelievable

### Moses – The Rhyming Haiku

Moses freed the slaves
parted the waves / took tablets
but never took shaves

### Why the First Murder Took Place

God preferred Abel's lamb
to Cain's potato wedges
The Almighty it appears
is not too keen on Veggies

### Abraham – Isaac's Goodfella's Ditty

It seems that the gentle Lord
is a bit like Joe Pesci

He said 'Stick the kid with a sword
No, I'm only messing'

## Lot – Weighing Up the Cost of Sin

Sodom and Gomorrah
What a horror
Lost a wife – not my fault
but gained a lifetime's supply of salt

## Samson – The Director's Cut

He put his head on his pillow
and there his hair was cut
Then he leant against a pillar
and the temple was kaput

## Jacob and Joseph

Jacob scams his dad and brother
by putting a goat's beard on
then loses his son Joseph
to a sibling goat-based con

## God as a 70s Parent

Remember when you cried as a kid
and your parent would shout
'Shut up or I'll give you
something to cry about'

Not happy with a problem?
God'll say 'Well here's a stye in your eye
no-one ever liked you
and soon you're going to die'

Then when you realise
you'll lose everything you had
on second thoughts that first problem
never seems so bad

## The Vicar's Wife

She'd only have sex on Sunday
if he wore his vicar's hat
So morning service and evensong
he said 'Amen to that'

## Jericho – The Sex Worker's Version

So these blokes come in from out of town
I said 'You looking for a good time?'

They said 'Can we hide in your roof?'
I said 'Is that a euphemism?'
They said 'No, we need to hide'

Anyway, they reckon they're
taking over the whole city next week
so I do a bit of a deal

Next day they're
outside the wall walking round like idiots
The following 5 days – same nonsense

End of the week they march round 7 times
then some blokes blow these horns
and you won't believe what happens next
The bloody walls only fall down don't they
You could have knocked me down with a feather

Before you know it these out-of-towners are in the city
killing everyone, even the oxen, the sheep, and the donkeys
Makes no sense
Everyone else is dead the animals belong to them now
but no, they stick it to the beasts anyway

Only me and my family get spared
because we had red cord up at the window
Well, us and the haberdashery
They were advertising a sale on red cord

## Nature's Not Your Friend

Nature's not your friend
it will kill you if it can
eat you, beat you or mistreat you
to shorten your life span

It'll do its damnedest to drown you
freeze or scorch your skin
suffocate or starve you
defeat you from within

Its beauty obscures an assassin
behind its bloodied back
Nature's not benign but
a mass murdering maniac

It will sting you or scratch you
Nature's not your friend
Whether you're buried or burnt
it'll get you in the end

## Ghost Writing a Poem I've Written Before

I'm plagiarising myself
second-hand insight by stealth

Counterfeiting my creativity
personalising petty larceny

Recycling and relabelling as new
like déjà voodoo

It's skull-sourced skullduggery
home-based humbuggery

Robbing my own grave
burgling a bygone brainwave

Memory embezzlement
inspiration zero percent

Leapfrogging the slog
cloning the back catalogue

These non-variations on a theme
making me my own meme

Not necessarily better
maybe more meta

I've got a nerve
reinventing my oeuvre

An accessory after the fact
I've become my very own tribute act

## Sunny Disposition

Even when you can't
see the sun it's comforting
to know it's still there

## Sigh-ku

Deadheading a flower
in bloom defeats the object
of the exercise

## Snipping a Digit

*(a cry-ku)*

Pruning my pinky
I know I am past my best
deadheading myself

## Fortune Favours the Bold Non-Bio

Our first date
she'll never forget
I took her for a spin
down the launderette

We sorted separates
on separate tables
I said I didn't
believe in labels

Her dress was hot
my shirt was cool
In a warm wash we
ignored the rules

I put in colours
I didn't think
All her whites
turned out pink
Prospects and pants
appeared to shrink

My smalls seemed smaller
my life seemed duller
until she said pink
was her favourite colour

## Humiliation

I've been here for years
hiding under hair
or behind the ear

or mistaken
for teenage spots
moles or other blemishes

Then I found the perfect place
The small of the back
Hard to see and harder to reach

Elbows, between toes
and the backs of legs
provide some cover

Armpits, heels
and behind the knee
all good sites

But now I'm all over legs
and arms using the weight
of numbers to confound

I've even dared skin
on the face
at the top of the cheek

I've got my ambition set on
those sacred places
around the eyes and mouth

the very end of the nose
making you a clown
or more of a clown

Then there's the backside
and beneath the pubes
and finally the genitalia

That would be
the cherry
on the icing

## Bespectacular

**a.**

Never drive in reading glasses
or run escalators in bifocals
Never swallow contact lenses
or you might affect your vocals

**b.**

My specs often have specks
I spend my time clearing them
or searching for the buggers
only to find I'm wearing them

**c.**

I have a spare pair somewhere
I keep them in their case
They're in there when they're
not appearing on my face

**d.**

I need my specs to find my specs
if I'm to answer all life's quizzes
Fumbling for my frames last night
I put on a pair of scissors

**e.**

I've invented prescription goggles
to wear in a snowstorm
They're double-glazed and guaranteed
to keep your eyeballs warm

**f.**

Don't call me 'foureyes'
trying to be jocular
I've two like you but behind glass
to assist on matters ocular

**g.**

I'd sooner be tasered
than have my eyes lasered

**h.**

Wear contacts? I'd sooner die
Bins are better than a poke in the eye

**i.**

As face furniture goes
frames make a fine addition
So if you can
form a plan
and see an optician

## Nights with White Statins

*(with apologies to The Moody Blues)*

Nights with white statins
Never reaching the end
Prescriptions written
Never meaning to spend

Heartbeats I'd always missed
With meat pies before
Just where the salt is
I can't say anymore

'Cause I love you
Yes, I love you
Oh, how I love you

Gazing at people
Burger in hand
Just what I'm going through
They can't understand

Some try to sell me
Diets they cannot defend
Just what you want for tea
Could well be your end

And I love you
Yes, I love you
Oh, how I love you
Oh, how I love you

## You Can Stick Your Vitamin D Where the Sun Don't Shine

Dad never bought bottled water
He knocked back builder's tea
Never dieted or detoxed
and lived to be 90

He never drank health drinks
He liked a bacon butty
Allergic to exercise
he'd just sit and watch TV

Preferred fry-ups to superfoods
Preferred Stilton to Brie
He never stayed at a spa
or swam in the cold North Sea

Dad wasn't mad for a fad
He never had vitamin D
He ate Lyons Maid not Lion's Mane
and lived to be 90

## Our Children

What would it take
for you to murder another
member of the human race?

How angry would they
have to make you?

Not to kill by mistake
but premeditated?

To break them
at a distance
or face to face
as if proximity
makes all the difference

What would it take
for you to murder a child?
What possible excuse
could you embrace?

What would it take
for you to stand by
and watch such murder
take place?

What would it take
for you to turn away
and erase the image?

What would it take
to speak up
to try to put on the brakes?

If you knew
in your heart
it was still happening

from you
who cherish humanity
what would it take?

## The Harrying of the North

*(twinned with Gaza)*

It's said the cruelty
devastation and famine
was but of its time

and that today such
genocide and destruction
would be a war crime

## Where is the World?

When your home
is torn down around you
it's hard to look

When your friends and
family are killed in front of you
it's hard to look

When your future
lies broken at your feet
it's hard to look

When everything you love
is dust
it's hard to look

When all you see
is the suffering
of those either side

it's hard to look
and even harder
to look away

## She's Top Drawer, I'm Sock Drawer

My partner's out of my league
although I try to be manly
She's Real Madrid
and I'm Accrington Stanley


## A Threesome with Donna Ashworth and Rupi Kaur

A threesome with Donna Ashworth and Rupi Kaur
would it be such a sin?
Sharing a shelf at every bookstore
instead of me in the bargain bin


## The Mixed-Up Chameleon in Love

If only I was younger, taller
with a better personality
fitter and more handsome
then she'd love the real me

## Never on a Sunday – Ode to Train Travel on the Sabbath

*(with apologies to Connie Francis)*


You can travel on a Monday
On Monday you might be quite impressed
but never travel on a Sunday
cos Sunday's the one day
God once chose to rest

Due to engineering works
prepare to enjoy the travel perks

It's not for the nervous
It's the Bus Replacement Service

They don't check your train ticket
no Rail Card need be displayed
No-one's going to board this bugger
unless they've already paid

Not to be pernickety
it's more a disservice
The bus is so rickety
you'll need a hip replacement service

Stopping at every stop
neither Mercury nor Hermes
can save you from a nightmare
lasting longer than Herpes

I'm dead in my seat
send no flowers
Gatwick to Hastings
in under 9 hours

## Nothing

I became invisible today
The dents in the bed where I slept
flattened out as I arose

I looked in the mirror
and there I was
gone

I brushed my teeth
and the toothpaste
became transparent as if by magic

I got dressed
and my clothes disappeared
which made no sense

I took off my scarf
and put it back on the hook
It reappeared

I pinched myself
in case I was
dreaming

The pain was real
but the reddening of my skin
was nowhere to be seen

I bumped into another man
He too had become invisible
We both apologised

Cars drove by with no-one in them
Babies cried
from empty prams

Only their tears could be seen
as they fell
on empty pillows

A highly visible man on TV
made promises of a future
that would never be seen

On the high street
No-one was reflected
in the shop windows

In the church
invisible people prayed
to an invisible God

## Kissing for the Over Sixties

In my teens I
used to dream
of the kisses
I was missing

In my twenties
I shared plenty

In my thirties and forties
they became
flirty and naughty

In my fifties
things became more thrifty

Now in my sixties
my lips still need their fixes

To be kissed at seventy
would be heavenly

## It Must Be Hard to Be Perfect

It must be hard to be so attractive
stunning with perfect skin
to be judged for your appearance
and not the character within

It must be hard to be so talented
where nothing is a task
it must be a bore having answers
for everything life asks

It must be hard to be so successful
that there's nothing left to prove
difficult not to stay in bed
once incentives are removed

It must be hard to be so famous
that everyone knows your face
where you can't have a day off
and disappear without a trace

It must be hard to be so sexy
the object of all desire
okay for half a day
but not for those who easily tire

It must be hard to be perfect
to have the cream and the jam
I wouldn't like to be perfect
I'm perfectly fine as I am

## The Next Poem on This Platform

I missed the last quatrain
whilst waiting for a sign
My thought process derailed
causing a delay on the line

## Colour Me Indifferent

Just got a Red Alert
Black Friday's almost here
but I'm having a Brown Friday
and poo-pooing the whole idea

## Tribute to the Scott Monument in Edinburgh

Looking a lot like Thunderbird Three
it seems to me to be wrong
as according to my memory
Scott was the pilot of Thunderbird One

## Alarmageddon

It's the end of the world again
with warnings that won't be ignored
All obliteration and oblivion
but I fear I'm getting bored

The brink of annihilation
has become the status quo
and the countdown to zero
seems to come and go

The rap of the rapture
The reaper at our door
The reckoning is beckoning
but we've seen it all before

The extinction of humanity
now just makes me numb
The Four Horsemen of the Apocalypse
have overstayed their welcome

Everyday is doomsday
Every gasp our last
The death spiral of decay
can't come round too fast

This constant catastrophe
is too much for my brain
I've no time for such prophesy
it's the end of the world again again

## Sympathy for the Devil – Updated

*(with apologies to The Rolling Stones)*


Please allow me to introduce myself
I'm a president with bad taste
I've been around for a long long time
and I've got a very orange face

I was 'round when "Hillary –
lock her up" was the refrain
Made damn sure America
bought making itself great again

Pleased to meet you
hope you guess my name
But what's puzzlin' you
is the nature of my biggly game

Stuck around The White House
when others saw it was a time for a change
Rioters tried to kill Nancy
made out Mike Pence was to blame

I rode a wave of the racist hate
when the right wing raged
and news became fake

Pleased to meet you
hope you guess my name, oh yeah
Ah, what's puzzling you
is the nature of my biggly game, ah yeah

I watched with glee (whoo-hoo)
while Twitter and TV (whoo-hoo)
fought the last decade (whoo-hoo)
For the truth they made (whoo-hoo)
I shouted out (whoo-hoo)
'Who killed the Honesty?' (whoo-hoo)
When after all (whoo-hoo)
it was down to me (whoo-hoo)

Let me please introduce myself (whoo-hoo, whoo-hoo)
I'm a president with bad taste (whoo-hoo, whoo-hoo)
and I laid traps for the Democrats (whoo-hoo, whoo-hoo)
who got killed in each swing state (whoo-hoo, whoo-hoo)

Pleased to meet you (whoo-hoo, whoo-hoo)
hope you guess my name, oh yeah (whoo-hoo, whoo-hoo)
but what's puzzlin' you (whoo-hoo)
is the nature of my biggly game, ah yeah (whoo-hoo, whoo-hoo)

Just as every lie is an alternative fact (whoo-hoo, whoo-hoo)
and all the KKK saints (whoo-hoo, whoo-hoo)
until I die just call me President (whoo-hoo, whoo-hoo)
'cause now I have no restraint (whoo-hoo, whoo-hoo)

So if you meet me, bow and curtsy (whoo-hoo, whoo-hoo)
have some sycophancy and bad taste (whoo-hoo, woo-hoo)
Use all your well-learned subservience (whoo-hoo, woo-hoo)
or I'll lay this world to waste, mmm yeah (whoo-hoo, woo-hoo)

Pleased to meet you (whoo-hoo, whoo-hoo)
hope you guess my name, oh yeah (whoo-hoo, whoo-hoo)
but what's puzzlin' you (whoo-hoo)
is the nature of my biggly game (whoo-hoo, whoo-hoo)

## Sometimes You Have to Play the Fool to Fool the Fool Who Thinks They are Fooling You

Time to drown an eel in water
to shade wood from the sun
to fence in a bush to keep a cuckoo captive
to tumble cheeses to Nottingham

They say there's one born every minute
'but there are more fools pass through Gotham
than remain in it'

## Flocking Freezing

*(or 'Knit Happens')*

I'm wearing winter knitwear
woven in the High Weald
If I wore anymore wool
they'd stand me in a field

Six pairs of socks, leg warmers
vest, shirt and cardigan
jacket, coat, gloves and hat
like a Lambswool Michelin Man

Under my jeans my wife's woollen tights
it's a wonder I don't start bleating
The truth is I'm sheepish
about turning on the central heating

Sewn into sheepskin slippers
I don't go out anymore
It's probably warmer outside
but I can't fit through the door

Merino scarf with earmuffs to match
I do look quite a state
A dog came in the house last night
and tried to steer me through a gate

Energy firms still try to fleece me
but I'm cosy till winter's done
Some say 'You – will turn into a ewe'
but it's the best way through baa none

## This Torch I Carry for You

I met her on a moonless night
in darkness devotion was born
I swore I'd carry this torch forever
but she snuffed it out at dawn

## Totally Blank Verse

Posterity may well say of me
*undiminished* when I'm departed
My best poems were left unfinished
The very best left unstarted

## An Unstarted Poem

*(blank verse from the collection 'Untitled')*

## An Interval

Take a break from heartache
A respite from shite

You don't need either
Book a breather

Whatever the causation
have a vacation

Forget life's flaws
Press pause

Quit for a bit
Put a peg in it

Just adjourn
Enjoy a sojourn

Be pragmatical
Opt for a sabbatical

Chill dude
Take an interlude

As for my status
I'm having a hiatus

## There's Something Not Right
## About Right Wing Marchers in Masks

If you believe you're right
I have to ask
why on earth
do you wear a mask?

If as you say
God is on your side
what in Heaven
have you got to hide?

If you are truly
the master race
why do you need
to cover your face?

## Shoe Zone and Vape Stores are No-one's Enemy

Looters with the flag of St George
professing Anglophilia
If you know your Muslim history
it's sadly too familia

## What Will Survive of Us is Not Gloves

There's no hats in Heaven or Hell
No one mentions wellies in their will
Lingerie may linger as landfill

There's no room in the box
for all your pants and socks
no call for them at charity shops

Your body will decompose
but the Good Lord knows
what will become of your spare clothes

There's no fashion parades
at the pearly gates
No need to take a packed suitcase

So whether your jeans get reused
whether someone walks in your old shoes
whether it all ends up as refuse

why should you care
Even your birthday suit may rip and tear
hopefully your soul will be elsewhere

Unless it surprises
I suspect Heaven fits all sizes

Let's celebrate all you used to hate
that you can't quite recall of late

All that's rotten
that you've forgotten

All the petty fears
from previous years

Each misgiving
faded by living

Issues
thrown out with the tissues

Gripes
gone with the wet-wipes

Uncertainties and queries
away with the fairies

Urgent troubles
burst like bubbles

Every woe
you've long let go

Apprehensions and tensions
now never mentioned

Gloom
left in some far-off room

Each grumble
that seemed to crumble

Disquiet and unease
now not even memories

Unhappiness and distress
now anyone's guess

That nagging doubt
that faded out

Those lost concerns
as the world turns

Let's be in no hurry
to remember each worry

The strand that time forgot
now replaced by a brand-new lot

## An Englishman's Home is His Shackle

Great to own your own home
your friends all say
as you're unblocking sewers
all through Christmas Day

## Christmas Lights Haiku Thank You

Thank you to all those
who decorate the cold night
with your Christmas lights

This selfless gesture
brightening the winter road
warms the journey home

## Debobbler – The Greatest Gift of All

Debobble all your cardigans
I never knew it was a thing to do
With all the bobbles from my cardies
I can now make another two

## Doggerel is Not Just for Christmas

I'm allergic to Christmas
I suffer from Santa fatigue
My body's become intolerant
to this bauble-clad blitzkrieg

Don't risk giving me a gift
No matter how you've wrapped it
the reaction you're going to get
is probably anaphylactic

Xmas gives me eczema
Carols makes me cringe
I'd sooner have a shot
of what they've got
in an anaesthetist's syringe

Keep all your presents
at Amazon's depository
When there's an anti-Noël vaccine
I might suggest a suppository

I find tinsel toxic
Mistletoe induces a malady
Turkey dinner makes me sick
I'd sooner something salady

So if you're Yuletide-sensitive
heed what the doctors say
Keep yourself to yourself
and take humbugs twice a day

**Winter Rose**

Not all flowers bloom
in summer / The best may still
be yet to blossom

**Out of Order Haiku**

My son in one hand
Moon in the other
The world is now in order

**Water Marks**

In its many forms
water migrates constantly
displaying textures

## The Culture of the Calendar and the Clock

Stopping up to hear
the midnight chimes of Big Ben
we welcome New Year

Despite weariness
we ignore our bodies and
mark out this moment

Tired animals
just sleep but we believe we
are so much smarter

We measure time like
syllables in a haiku
and abide by it

## Wedding Gift

I bought a beach for Debra
for when our souls enjoin
but she left me at the altar
with my abandoned groyne


## Do You Believe in Sex After Marriage?

As you get older
sex becomes like a
Christmas dinner I fear

It takes too long to get ready
is all over in seconds
and happens once a year


## Talking to Ange on Our Wedding Anniversary

I said 'I recall when love first took hold
I know you loved me then
but will you love me when I'm old?'
And she said 'What do you mean when?'

## Stacking Logs

Like with any mundane task
you find you talk to yourself

Develop a system

See how many logs
you can carry
at the same time

Stack the heavy logs together
near the door
the lighter logs
further over

Start defining the wood
by shape as well as size

The short squat ones
The long round ones

You take pride in
building up the wall evenly

and end with the scraps
hoping the rain holds off

and telling yourself
people pay good money
for this sort of exercise

Not one log lit as yet
and you're already warm

## Rebuilding this Poem

Oooooh it's going to cost you!
What cowboy built this?

All the parts don't match up
There's Capital letters and lower case ad Hoc

I'm surprised it's held together this long
The rhymes are all in the wrong place

The Meter is inconsistent
at best
Some of the words just don't fit
And they've used different size stanzas

There's hardly any alliteration to speak of
It's a mess at the moment to be honest

I'm very busy this next few days
Renovating a Shakespearean sonnet
But I could look at it

A week a Wednesday if we can do cash

In the meantime
I'd cover it over
With a bit of post-modern irony

Before it takes someone's eye out

# You're Not the First Clown That's Been Let Down

*(a consolation poem to those unexpectedly ditched)*

You're not the first buffoon
with a burst balloon

Not the first bumpkin
to have someone dump him

Not the first galoot
to get the boot

Not the first clodhopper
to come a cropper

Not the first chump
to hit a bump

Not the first schmuck
to come unstuck

Not the first bonehead
to be misled

Not the first goofball
to take a fall

Not the first palooka
hit by a bazooka

Not the first moron
Lady Luck went sore on

Not the first bozo
the last to know

Not the first daft bastard
flabbergasted

## Beyond the Dark

It's dark beyond the glass
but beyond the dark
there's you

So the night holds no fear
it's just something
we pass through

And if you look out your window
and wonder what is there

know beyond the dark
love is waiting for you here

## The Case for the Defence

I fell in love with a lawyer
but as marriage beckoned
I found when I'd court her
she'd bill me by the second

She made me sign a pre-nup
made me swear on *The Bible*
I wrote her a love poem
now she's suing me for libel

She's taken out a restraining order
from which I now infer
I'm not allowed to read poetry
within two million miles of her

She's in love with litigation
so things went from bad to worse
Today she sent me a summons
disclaiming custody of this verse

## Surprise Me

For my hundredth birthday
the best present you could bring
is that all children are born equal
You can keep your card from the King


## Toast

Until the final whistle blows
may you play the game to win it
with all the pace and passion
of the very first minute


## On Seeing a Photo of My Son

'He's got my nose'
I told my wife
'But' I said 'The fact is

his smile is better'
And she said
'He's had more practise'

## Does the NHS Have Shares in Vodaphone?

I've written a novel called *Waiting*
which I've typed whilst trying
to get a doctor's appointment
to delay myself from dying

No sign of a medic yet
but all things being equal
before I see my GP
I should finish the sequel

The story is autobiographical
true in every word I've penned
And the way things are looking
the hero dies in the end

I may make it a series
if my health's not too diminished
but more likely an epic poem
one that's left un

I let my lad watch *MTV 80s*
but with some compunction
having since seen the ads
for erectile disfunction

He doesn't need a blue pill
like most other young lads
he won't be writing his will
or buying Tena pads

He's led a sheltered life
due to his natural shyness
He's no need to know right now
about vaginal dryness

## The Schoolboy's Tale

I had a crush on my teacher
our love it defied convention
We spent so much time together
as I was always getting detention

I wrote her a love poem
listing all my passion entailed
She read it then gave it back
She'd marked it F for failed

In lessons I would daydream
her lips I'd imagine tasting
but she'd bring me back to class saying
'It's your own time that you're wasting'

Today I declared my undying love
I didn't know what I was doing
I said 'I worship your every word'
and she said 'Are you chewing?'

I proposed marriage there and then
my heart could beat no faster
And in truth, that's why I'm here
to see you today Headmaster

## Squeak in My Shoe

*(à la Dr. Seuss)*

I've a squeak in my shoe
a creak with each stride
When I step it sounds
like a mouse has just died

You can hear me coming
like a small child's toy
There's nothing on earth
more guaranteed to annoy

I've lost all my cool
my decorum is shot
and all because of
this squeak that I've got

It's what's held me back
all the things I could do
If only I hadn't
a squeak in my shoe

I'm fine when sitting
I'm okay when I stand
but when I walk I sound
like a shit one-man band

## Appointment with Dr Frankenstein

I went for my Well Man test
it's a routine thing to do
They said 'Well man, to be honest
if you were a horse we'd shoot you'

When I asked for a second opinion
I could hear the doctor scoffing
Then a very strange minion
helped me into a coffin

You're only good for spare parts
said the medic unimpressed
He was a man after my own heart
or anything he could harvest

My hands would come in handy
My ears earmarked for a friend
My elbows he said were dandy
and to his will would bend

My eyes would see him right
On my feet he'd stand his ground
but my brains were, to be polite
not many to the pound

He said recycling of the poor
was part of a new health scheme
Then I awoke and he was no more
it was all just a terrible dream

So do go to the Well Man test
they'll take your blood for starters
But if they privatise the NHS
they'll have your guts for garters

## An Alphabet of Storms

I am off balance
from the flood in my ears

Other fluids affect my pulse
weighting my eyes

Confusion sears my core
with an ocean of tears

If these waters don't quieten
I fear I will be lost to the tide

## The Last Laugh

What will be my final expression?
Will it be my resting face?
Or will my features truly relax
and form a brand-new shape?

Will I appear disappointed?
Will it depend on my demise?
Maybe bemused by the afterlife?
Or pleasantly surprised?

Will undertakers manipulate my muscles
into a grin quite enigmatic?
Or on seeing what it's all been about
will my smile be automatic?

Perhaps as a last laugh
in my will – to avoid doubt
I could demand an open coffin
and that they stick my tongue out

## Imposter Syndrome

I shouldn't be writing this poem
I'm not really a poet at all
There's no assonance or alliteration
I've not got the wherewithal

The rhythm's down the pan
It doesn't really scan
Lines are too short
or go on and on and on and on for as long as they possibly can

It seems to me you see
and I feel you will agree
this cannot be poetry
It doesn't always rhyme

## You're the Miss Piggy to My Kermit

You're the Torvill to my Dean
the knife to my fork
the Florence to my Machine
the Mindy to my Mork

You're the Morecambe to my Wise
the tune to my song
the burger to my fries
the ping to my pong

You're the Bacall to my Bogart
the cure to my disease
the arrow to my heart
the macaroni to my cheese

You're the Wilma to my Fred
the chocolate factory to my Charlie
the butter to my bread
the melted clocks to my Dali

You're the Lois Lane to my Superman
the Chow to my Chow Chow
the Duran to my Duran
the Bow to my Wow Wow

You're the muse to my ballad
the ink to my pen
the Caesar to my salad
the Deirdre to my Ken

## This is Not Something We Talk About

There's a difference between loving
and feeling loved by someone

In the giving and the receiving

Looking back on your life
I know you will have given love

It comes naturally
but what is harder
is the receiving of love

That's not to say others
have not loved you

But more often than not
we seem reluctant
or scared to believe
we are loved

We believe we may have been
liked or respected
or even considered a friend

But feeling loved
like joy or Heaven
can feel distant, fleeting or other

Not for us

Whether once or twice
or many times
for a moment or longer even

Not for us

We judge ourselves sometimes
in terms of success and achievements
or the lack of them

Sometimes we may consider
the love we have given
but seldom do we consider
our own feelings
as though they are of
no significance

Looking back on your life
I hope at times
you have felt loved

And looking forward
I hope
you will feel loved

## Tomorrow is Easier to See in Retrospect

The future is a jigsaw puzzle
whose size we're only guessing
We can't see the full picture
and some of the pieces are missing

The number of pieces keep increasing
Some bits don't seem to fit
Some pieces are in the wrong place
Some aren't even painted yet

Patient pragmatism is the key
to make the future less tense
Only once the box arrives
will the puzzle all make sense

## Ten Thousand Steps

I catch my breath
amongst gravestones
whose words are worn away
by countless winters

Crocus and daffodils
announce a new spring

Thoughts of granite and gravity
weigh heavy as I circle the glen
and climb past the quarry

The steep inclines I walked
when younger now daunt
Light glances off teased water

The breeze is only enough
to sway the smaller branches

On my return to the churchyard I notice
some of the stone markers are leaning back
as though relaxing in the midday sun

I don't think I can face another salad

and I wonder how many summers
we have left

I've written too many poems
some playful
some with greater intent

and yet not one good enough
to fulfil the yearning
I felt as a boy to create

from within my core
something of beauty
and worth

that would outlive
these small concerns

A love letter
or a suicide note

to use as a shield
or a bridge

to defy the coming night
contain the stars
crowd the silence
calm the absence of God
and to wipe away the tears

There is little of me
left to love

What little there is
is here
in these hidden prayers

Maybe together they may form
a structure taller than
this pauper's grave

or perhaps in the passion
I have somewhere and somehow
happened upon
a moment of inspiration
and substance
for you to discover

That is my hope

My victory or defeat
rests within your hands

flapjackpress.co.uk